A+
books

WORLD OF COLORS

Guatemala in Colors

by Ann Stalcup

Consultant: Colin M. MacLachlan
John Christy Barr
Distinguished Professor of History
Tulane University
New Orleans, Louisiana

Capstone
press®

Mankato, Minnesota

The setting sun paints these Mayan pyramids **orange** in northern Guatemala. The Maya have lived in Guatemala for thousands of years. Almost half of Guatemala's people are Mayan.

3

Children in **white** uniforms visit Mayan ruins. Besides history, students study math, science, reading, writing, and art. Mayan students must also learn Spanish.

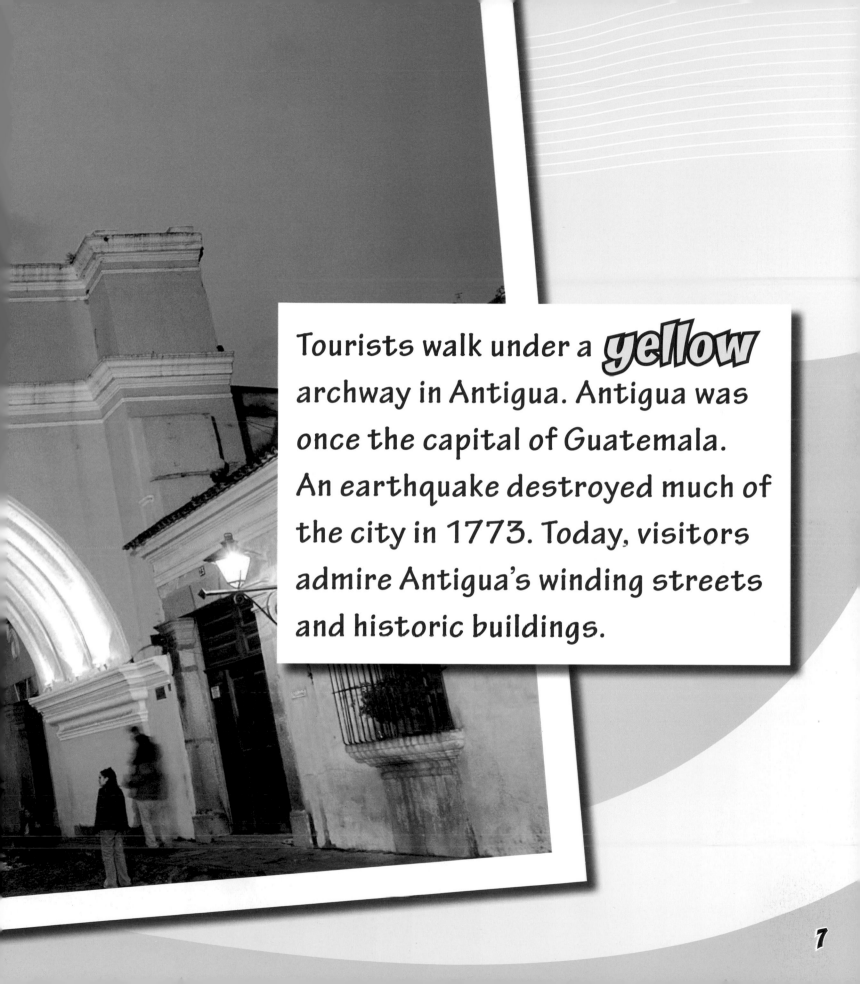

Tourists walk under a *yellow* archway in Antigua. Antigua was once the capital of Guatemala. An earthquake destroyed much of the city in 1773. Today, visitors admire Antigua's winding streets and historic buildings.

A Guatemalan soccer player in a **blue** uniform runs down the field. Soccer is a very popular sport in Guatemala. Many families go to soccer games on weekends.

Ripe **red** coffee berries grow well in the cool Guatemalan highlands. The berries are picked, dried, and roasted. Guatemalan coffee is sold to countries around the world.

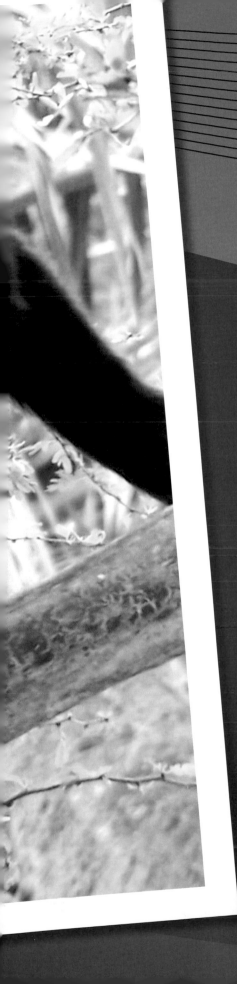

Black howler monkeys live in Guatemala's rain forests. They eat fruit, leaves, and flowers. Their strange howls can be heard from miles away!

13

Many Mayan families live in **white** homes with grass roofs. The walls are built with adobe bricks. The Maya make the bricks with mud and straw. The hot sun dries the bricks.

Green bananas grow well on Guatemala's Pacific and Caribbean coasts. Bananas need lots of rain and warm weather to grow. Bunches of bananas are shipped to other countries.

Fried **brown** buñuelos are a favorite holiday treat. They are made from flour, water, eggs, and butter. A sprinkle of powdered sugar makes them extra sweet.

Green, **red**, and **white** quetzal birds live in Guatemala's rain forests. They eat fruit, lizards, and insects. The quetzal is the national bird of Guatemala.

Men wearing **purple** robes walk in a Semana Santa parade. Semana Santa parades are held the week before Easter. Flowers, fruit, and branches decorate the streets. Families go to church.

A Mayan woman weaves strips of cloth with **blue** thread. The strips are used to make shirts, skirts, and pants. Dyes from plants and minerals give the thread its rich color. Many women sell the clothing they make at markets.

These Mayan children wear **blue** and **red** clothing. Each village has its own special clothing design. In cities, Guatemalans wear store-bought clothing.

FACTS about Guatemala

Capital City: Guatemala City

Population: 13,002,206

Official Language: Spanish

Common Phrases

English	Spanish	Pronunciation
hello	hola	(OH-lah)
good-bye	adiós	(ah-dee-OHS)
yes	sí	(SEE)
no	no	(NO)

Map

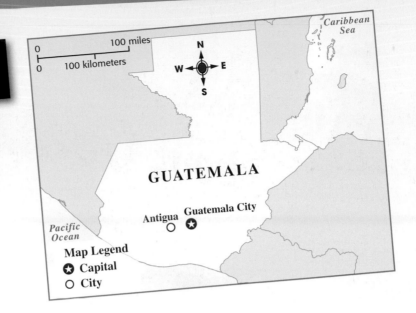

Flag

Money

Guatemalan money is called the quetzal. One quetzal equals 100 centavos.

Glossary

adobe brick (uh-DOH-bee BRIK) — a brick made of mud and straw and dried in the sun

buñuelo (boon-u-WAY-low) — a fried pastry treat made of dough

highland (HYE-luhnd) — an area with mountains or hills

Maya (MY-uh) — a member of an American Indian people who lives in southern Mexico and Central America

mineral (MIN-ur-uhl) — a material found in nature that is not an animal or a plant

parade (puh-RADE) — a line of people, bands, cars, or floats that travels through a town; parades celebrate special events and holidays.

pyramid (PIHR-uh-mid) — a stone monument

quetzal (ket-SAHL) — a red, green, and white bird; the quetzal is the national bird of Guatemala.

rain forest (RAYN FOR-ist) — a thick forest where a great deal of rain falls

Semana Santa (say-MAH-nah SAHN-tuh) — the week before Easter; Easter is the Christian holiday on which people remember the death of Jesus.

Read More

Aboff, Marcie. *Guatemala ABCs: A Book about the People and Places of Guatemala.* Country ABCs. Minneapolis: Picture Window Books, 2006.

Englar, Mary. *Guatemala: A Question and Answer Book.* Questions and Answers. Countries. Mankato, Minn.: Capstone Press, 2006.

Internet Sites

FactHound offers a safe, fun way to find Internet sites related to this book. All of the sites on FactHound have been researched by our staff.

Here's how:

1. Visit www.facthound.com

2. Choose your grade level.

3. Type in this book ID **1429617004** for age-appropriate sites. You may also browse subjects by clicking on letters, or by clicking on pictures and words.

4. Click on the **Fetch It** button.

FactHound will fetch the best sites for you!

Index

A+ Books are published by Capstone Press,
151 Good Counsel Drive, P.O. Box 669, Mankato, Minnesota 56002.
www.capstonepress.com

1 2 3 4 5 6 13 12 11 10 09 08

Library of Congress Cataloging-in-Publication Data
Stalcup, Ann, 1935–
    Guatemala in colors / by Ann Stalcup.
    p. cm. — (A+ books. World of colors)
    Summary: "Simple text and striking photographs present Guatemala, its culture,
and its geography" — Provided by publisher.
    Includes bibliographical references and index.
    ISBN-13: 978-1-4296-1700-0 (hardcover)
    ISBN-10: 1-4296-1700-4 (hardcover)
    1. Guatemala — Juvenile literature. [1. Guatemala.] I. Title. II. Series.
F1463.2.S73 2009
972.81 — dc22   2008005272

Credits
Megan Peterson, editor; Veronica Bianchini, designer; Wanda Winch, photo researcher

Photo Credits
Alamy/Robert Fried, 2–3; Art Life Images/age fotostock/Kevin Schafer, 21; Capstone
Press/Karon Dubke, 18–19; Dreamstime/Christopher Marin, 1; Getty Images Inc./
Stephen Dunn, 9; The Image Works/Bill Bachmann, 6–7; The Image Works/Bob
Daemmrich, 5; iStockphoto/Judy Tillinger, 25; One Mile Up, Inc., 29 (flag); Paul Baker,
29 (coins); Photri MicroStock, 15; Richard Sutherland, 29 (banknote); Shutterstock/
Don Long, 16–17; Shutterstock/Jaana Piira, 12; Shutterstock/Sandra A. Dunlap,
10–11; South American Pictures/Robert Francis, 22–23; South American Pictures/Tony
Morrison, cover, 26–27

Note to Parents, Teachers, and Librarians
This World of Colors book uses full-color photographs and a nonfiction format to
introduce children to basic topics in the study of countries. *Guatemala in Colors*
is designed to be read aloud to a pre-reader or to be read independently by an
early reader. Photographs help listeners and early readers understand the text
and concepts discussed. The book encourages further learning by including the
following sections: Facts about Guatemala, Glossary, Read More, Internet Sites,
and Index. Early readers may need assistance using these features.